Searchlight
BOOKS

What
Is a
Food Web?

Lake and Pond Food Webs

in Action

Paul Fleisher

Lerner Publications Company
Minneapolis

Lerner Publications Company
A division of Lerner Publishing Group, Inc.
241 First Avenue North
Minneapolis, MN 55401 U.S.A.

Website address: www.lernerbooks.com

Library of Congress Cataloging-in-Publication Data

Fleisher, Paul.
    Lake and pond food webs in action / by Paul Fleisher.
       p.   cm. — (Searchlight books™—what is a food web?)
    Includes index.
    ISBN 978–1–4677–1256–9 (lib. bdg. : alk. paper)
    ISBN 978–1–4677–1776–2 (eBook)
    1. Lake ecology—Juvenile literature. 2. Lake plants—Juvenile literature. 3. Lake animals—Juvenile literature. I. Title.
    QH541.5.L3F58 2013
    577.63—dc23   2012034112

Manufactured in the United States of America
1 – BP – 7/15/13

Contents

A LAKE OR POND FOOD WEB

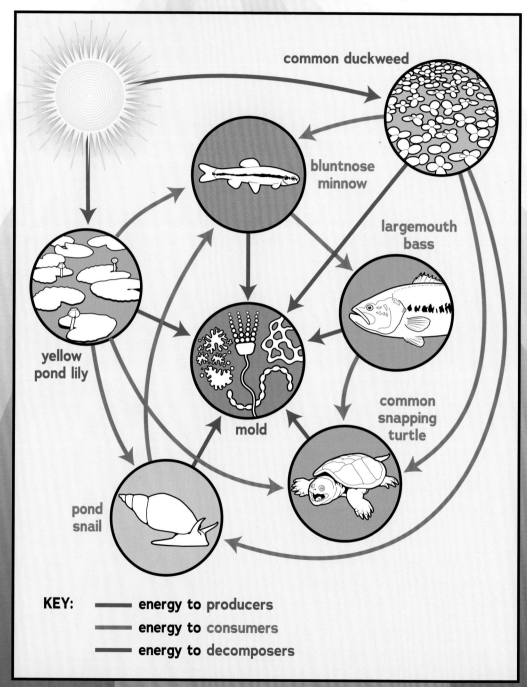

common duckweed

bluntnose minnow

largemouth bass

yellow pond lily

mold

common snapping turtle

pond snail

KEY:
- energy to producers
- energy to consumers
- energy to decomposers

Chapter 1

LAKES AND PONDS

A great blue heron wades in a lake. The tall bird stands very still. Then it stabs its beak into the water. It catches a fish and swallows it. Herons hunt in the shallow water of lakes and ponds. Many creatures live in the water. Others live along the water's edge. Plants grow in the water too. Insects fly above it.

This bird is a great blue heron. It has caught a fish. Where do herons hunt for food?

A young white-tailed deer has come to a pond to drink water.

Environments

Lakes and ponds are some of Earth's most important environments. An environment is the place where any creature lives. The environment includes the air, the soil, and the weather. It includes plants and animals too.

Plants and animals in lakes and ponds depend on one another. Some animals eat plants. Other animals are meat eaters. They eat other animals. When plants and animals die, they decay. They break down into chemicals. Some of the chemicals are called nutrients. Living things need nutrients to grow.

Many fish eat meat. This bass is eating a frog.

Food Chains and Energy

Energy moves from one living thing to another. A food chain shows how the energy moves. The energy for life comes from the sun. Plants store the sun's energy in their leaves, stems, and roots. When an animal eats a plant, the animal gets some of the sun's energy from the plant. The energy moves farther along the food chain each time one living thing eats another.

A fish is watching a frog. If the fish eats the frog, the fish will get energy from the frog.

Lakes have many food chains. Imagine that a tadpole eats a plant. Then a sunfish eats the tadpole. A heron eats the sunfish. When the heron dies, a crayfish eats its body. The sun's energy goes from the plant to the tadpole. Then it passes to the sunfish. Then it goes to the heron. Then it goes to the crayfish.

A TADPOLE IS A YOUNG FROG.
THIS TADPOLE IS EATING A PLANT.

Food Webs

But sunfish don't eat only tadpoles. They eat insects and minnows too. Herons eat many different kinds of fish. And crayfish eat many kinds of living and dead animals.

An environment's food web is made up of many food chains. A food web shows how all living things depend on one another for food.

This sunfish is eating a smaller fish.

Chapter 2

LAKE AND POND PLANTS

Green plants use sunlight to make food. Because plants produce food, they are called producers. Plants also make oxygen. Oxygen is a gas in the air. All animals need oxygen to breathe.

Water lilies are green plants that grow in lakes and ponds. How do green plants use sunlight?

Making Food and Oxygen

The way plants make food and oxygen is called photosynthesis. Plants need carbon dioxide, sunlight, and water for photosynthesis. Carbon dioxide is a gas in the air. A plant's leaves take in carbon dioxide and sunlight. The plant's roots take in water. The plant uses energy from sunlight to turn the carbon dioxide and water into sugar and starch. Sugar and starch are the plant's own food. The plant stores this food in its leaves and roots.

HOW PHOTOSYNTHESIS WORKS

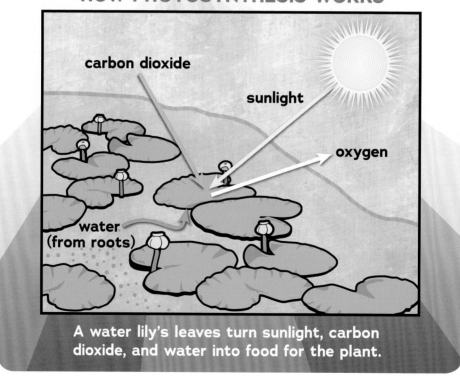

carbon dioxide

sunlight

oxygen

water
(from roots)

A water lily's leaves turn sunlight, carbon dioxide, and water into food for the plant.

As the plant makes food, it also makes oxygen. The oxygen goes into the air and the water. Animals breathe in the oxygen. They breathe out carbon dioxide. Plants use the carbon dioxide to make more food.

This is a young red-spotted newt. It has gills behind its eyes. The newt uses its gills to breathe oxygen that is in the water.

Kinds of Plants

Algae are tiny plants. They float in the water. Algae are the most important producers in the pond. But most algae are so small we can't see them.

Sometimes algae piles up in thick mats. You can see bubbles of oxygen in this algae mat. The algae made the oxygen through photosynthesis.

Larger plants live in lakes too. Duckweed plants float on top of the water. They have short roots. The roots hang in the water. They do not grow down into the soil at the bottom of the lake.

Many green duckweed plants are floating in this lake. The duckweed plants are tiny compared to the water lily leaf and the butterfly.

The roots of water lilies reach down through the water. They grow into the mud at the bottom. Water lilies have light, spongy leaves. Their leaves float on the water's surface.

Other plants grow in shallow water along the shore. Their roots grow in the mud at the bottom of the pond. Wild rice is a kind of grass. It grows in shallow water. Cattails grow at the edge of the pond too.

Plants in the Fall

Some plants die each fall, when the weather gets colder. But before they die, they make seeds. The next spring, new plants grow from the seeds.

Other plants turn brown in the fall, but they don't die. Their roots live through the winter. Their seeds live too. In the spring, new leaves grow from the plants' roots. And new plants grow from the seeds.

This lake is in a place that has cold winters. The top of the water has frozen into ice. But plants and animals are still living under the ice.

Chapter 3

LAKE AND POND PLANT EATERS

Animals are called consumers. *Consume* means "eat." Animals that eat only plants are called herbivores. Energy from the sun is stored inside plants. When an animal eats a plant, it gets the sun's energy.

Pond snails eat algae and other kinds of plants. What are some other plant-eating animals that live in lakes and ponds?

Small Herbivores

Some herbivores are tiny. Look at a jar full of pond water. You can see hundreds of tiny specks. The specks are swimming. Each one is a little animal. Copepods and daphnia are tiny animals that look like shrimp. Copepods and daphnia eat algae.

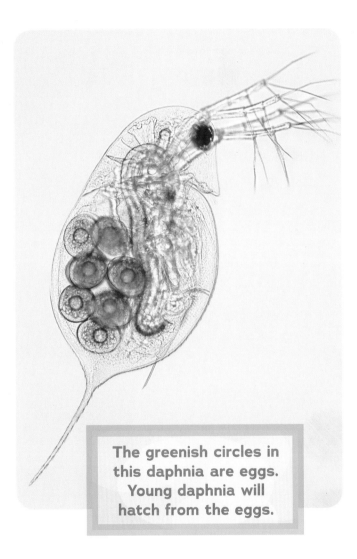

The greenish circles in this daphnia are eggs. Young daphnia will hatch from the eggs.

Many insects live in or near water. Mayflies live near lakes and ponds. They lay their eggs in the water. Baby insects hatch out of the eggs. They live in the water. The young mayflies eat algae.

Larger animals also eat lake plants. Snails have rough tongues. They use their tongues to scrape algae off rocks.

Young mayflies have gills on their backs for breathing underwater.

Fish, Birds, and Other Animals

Some fish are herbivores. Shiners and minnows eat plants. Carp grow large by eating underwater plants.

Some birds are herbivores too. Mallard ducks and Canada geese eat plants. In the fall, some lake plants produce seeds. Many birds feast on the seeds.

Some carp are very big. They can be longer than a yardstick.

Other animals are herbivores too. Muskrats and beavers live in lakes and ponds. Muskrats eat roots, seeds, stems, and leaves. Beavers eat twigs and bark. Deer come to lakes to drink water. They eat plants growing along the shore.

THIS ANIMAL IS A MUSKRAT.
MUSKRATS ARE GOOD SWIMMERS.

Chapter 4

LAKE AND POND MEAT EATERS

Some lake and pond creatures eat meat. These animals are called carnivores. Carnivores eat animals. But they need plants too. Carnivores get energy by eating animals that have eaten plants.

Many fish eat meat. What do we call animals that eat meat?

Insects, Frogs, and Fish

Many insects are carnivores. Dragonflies fly above lakes and ponds. They hunt mosquitoes and other flying insects. Young dragonflies live in the water. They eat insects too.

This dragonfly has caught a mosquito.

Frogs are carnivores. They catch insects and other small animals. Water snakes swim through the water. They hunt for fish and frogs.

Many fish are carnivores. Bass eat smaller fish. They also eat insects and frogs.

WATER SNAKES ARE GOOD SWIMMERS. THEY EAT FISH, FROGS, AND TADPOLES.

Birds and Bats

Many kinds of birds live near lakes and ponds. Kingfishers perch on branches near the water. Then they dive into the water. They catch small fish in their beaks.

Kingfishers eat mostly fish. But they also hunt crayfish, snails, and other small animals.

At night, bats fly over lakes and ponds. They catch and eat flying insects. Some bats can even catch small fish swimming in the water.

At night, bats fly close to the water to catch fish.

Eating Plants and Animals

Some animals are omnivores. Omnivores are animals that eat both plants and animals. Catfish are omnivores. They swim at the bottom of lakes and ponds. Catfish eat plants. They hunt for fish, insects, and worms. They also eat animals that have died and fallen to the bottom.

Catfish eat mostly meat. But they also eat underwater plants, algae, and seeds that fall into the water.

Raccoons are also omnivores. Raccoons often live near lakes and ponds. They look for food in and near the water. Raccoons eat fruit and berries. They also eat frogs, snakes, crayfish, and bird eggs.

This raccoon is eating a fish.

Chapter 5

LAKE AND POND DECOMPOSERS

All living things die. When plants and animals die, they decay. They break down into nutrients. Living things called decomposers help dead things decay. Decomposers feed on dead plants and animals.

Dead leaves have fallen into this pond. What will happen to them?

Nature's Recycling Crew

Decomposers are nature's recycling crew. Dead plants and animals sink to the bottom of the pond. Decomposers feed on them. Nutrients from the dead plants and animals become part of the mud on the bottom. The nutrients go back into the pond. Then other living things can use the nutrients.

Decomposers are very important. Without them, lakes and ponds would become filled with dead plants and animals. Then no new plants could grow. Animals would run out of food.

This dead mosquito is covered with mold. The mold is breaking down the mosquito's body.

Bacteria are the most important decomposers in lakes and ponds. Bacteria are too tiny for us to see. Millions of bacteria live in the water. Millions more live in the mud at the bottom.

Some animals eat plants and animals that have died. These animals are called scavengers. Catfish are scavengers. Crayfish are scavengers too.

CRAYFISH LOOK LIKE SMALL LOBSTERS.

Becoming Dry Land

Each year, plants die and fall into the water. Decomposers turn the dead plants into mud. Ponds and lakes slowly fill with mud. The water gets shallower. After many, many years, lakes and ponds may become dry land.

This wetland is a bog. It formed when moss grew on a lake's surface. After many years, the bog may become dry land.

Chapter 6

PEOPLE AND LAKES

People go fishing and boating on ponds and lakes. People build towns and cities near lakes. People need water to drink and to wash with. They add chemicals to the lake water to make sure it's clean. Then they pump it through pipes to people's homes.

Many people like to go boating on lakes. What are some other ways people use lakes?

Too Many Nutrients

Plants and animals that live in lakes need nutrients to grow. But sometimes lakes get too many nutrients. People put fertilizer on lawns or farms. Rain can wash fertilizer into lakes. Fertilizer has nutrients that plants need. It makes lawns green. It helps farm crops grow. But fertilizer makes algae grow too fast.

Too much algae is growing in this pond.

When too much algae grows in a lake, the water becomes cloudy. Underwater plants can't get enough light to grow. When the extra algae dies, bacteria break it down. Many kinds of bacteria use oxygen when they break down dead plants. As the bacteria break down the algae, they use most of the oxygen in the water. Fish in the lake may not have enough oxygen to breathe. The fish may die.

This lake doesn't have enough oxygen for fish to breathe. Many fish have died.

Treat with Care

Lakes and ponds are important. We must take care of them. If we don't, the water won't be good to drink. It won't be clean enough to swim in. It won't be a good home for plants and animals. People must treat ponds and lakes with care.

This snapping turtle lives in a lake in Florida.

Glossary

algae: simple plants that have no leaves, stems, or roots. Algae grow in water or on wet surfaces.

bacteria: tiny living things that are made up of just one cell. Bacteria can be seen only under a microscope.

carnivore: an animal that eats meat

consumer: a living thing that eats other living things. Animals are consumers.

decay: to break down

decomposer: a living thing that feeds on dead plants and animals

environment: the place where any creature lives. An environment includes the air, soil, weather, plants, and animals in a place.

food chain: the way energy moves from the sun to a plant, then to a plant eater, then to a meat eater, and finally to a decomposer

food web: many food chains connected together. A food web shows how all living things in a place need one another for food.

herbivore: an animal that eats only plants

nutrient: a chemical that living things need to grow

omnivore: an animal that eats both plants and meat

oxygen: a gas in the air. All animals need oxygen to breathe.

photosynthesis: the way green plants use energy from sunlight to make their own food out of carbon dioxide and water

producer: a living thing that makes its own food. Plants are producers.

scavenger: an animal that eats dead plants and animals

Learn More about Lakes, Ponds, and Food Webs

Books

Hauth, Katherine B. *What's for Dinner? Quirky, Squirmy Poems from the Animal World.* Watertown, MA: Charlesbridge, 2011. Squirm at the realities of how the animal world catches food, eats it, and then becomes dinner in these twenty-nine gross, cool, and funny poems.

Mooney, Carla. *Explore Rivers and Ponds!: With 25 Great Projects.* White River Junction, VT: Nomad Press, 2012. Learn about the creatures of freshwater habitats with these hands-on ecology activities.

Wojahn, Rebecca Hogue, and Donald Wojahn. *An Estuary Food Chain: A Who-Eats-What Adventure in North America.* Minneapolis: Lerner Publications Company, 2010. What you choose to eat shapes your fate in this fun, interactive story about food chains.

Websites

Chain Reaction
http://www.ecokids.ca/pub/eco_info/topics/frogs/chain_reaction/index.cfm#
Play this food chain game to find out what happens if one link is taken out.

Explore the Life of a Pond
http://library.thinkquest.org/04oct/00228
Explore the animals and plants that live in a pond, and find activities to help you investigate a pond near you!

Kids Do Ecology: Freshwater Biome
http://kids.nceas.ucsb.edu/biomes/freshwater.html
Learn what lives in a freshwater ecosystem, and read about why these habitats are so important for animals, plants, and people.

LERNER
SOURCE™

Expand learning beyond the printed book. Download free, complementary educational resources for this book from our website, www.lernerresource.com.

Index

Photo Acknowledgments

The images in this book are used with the permission of: Zeke Smith, pp. 4, 12; © Gregg Williams/Shutterstock.com, p. 5; © iStockphoto.com/PhotosbyAndy, p. 6; © Gary Meszaros/Visuals Unlimited, Inc., pp. 7, 13; © Wally Eberhart/Visuals Unlimited, Inc., p. 8; © Dave Pressland/FLPA/Photo Researchers, Inc., p. 9; © Frei/ARCO/naturepl.com, p. 10; © iStockphoto.com/Peter Mukherjee, p. 11; © iStockphoto.com/Julie Weiss, p. 14; © FotoVeto/Shutterstock.com, p. 15; © George Grall/National Geographic/Getty Images, p. 16; © Anna Rutkovskaya/Dreamstime.com, p. 17; © Stephen Dalton/Minden Pictures, p. 18; © Wim van Egmond/Visuals Unlimited, Inc., p. 19; © Cubo Images/SuperStock, p. 20; © Vladvitek/Deposit Photos, p. 21; © Mirceax/Dreamstime.com, p. 22; © Age Fotostock/SuperStock, p. 23; © Bill Beatty/Visuals Unlimited, Inc., p. 24; © Jan Van Arkel/Minden Pictures, p. 25; © Photographs by Les Piccolo/Flickr/Getty Images, p. 26; © Bruce and Nancy Cushing/Visuals Unlimited, Inc., p. 27; © Ken Lucas/Visuals Unlimited, Inc., p. 28; © Danita Delimont/Gallo Images/Getty Images, p. 29; © IS stock/Thinkstock, p. 30; © Glenn Oliver/Visuals Unlimited, Inc., p. 31; © Olgysha/Shutterstock.com, p. 32; © Zeljko Radojko/Shutterstock.com, p. 33; © Ariel Skelley/Blend Images/Getty Images, p. 34; © IStockphoto/Thinkstock, p. 35; © iStockphoto.com/Michael Hendricks, p. 36; © Bill Curtsinger/National Geographic/Getty Images, p. 37.

Front cover: © iStockphoto.com/Megan Lorenz.

Main body text set in Adrianna Regular 14/20.
Typeface provided by Chank.